PRAYERS

Finding Power in Vulnerability

A.J. ROBERT

Published by: Limitless Consulting Solutions, LLC

Cover design: WordSugar Designs

Hardback ISBN: 978-1-7374025-0-3

Paperback ISBN: 978-1-7374025-1-0

E-book ISBN: 978-1-7374025-2-7

Preface

To the Reader,

Thank you for purchasing, borrowing—or even stealing—my book. My hope is that it will bless you immensely; crafting it has certainly blessed me.

This book is a series of prayers I either prayed or imagined one might pray to the Lord when experiencing the many ebbs and flows of life. These prayers gave way to creating a deeper relationship with God, and they exemplify the very vulnerability necessary to access His presence.

I wrote this book in the midst of trials, death, pain, heartbreak, remorse, guilt, affliction, desperation, loneliness, and...faith. It was in every one of these moments that the Lord kept me and sheltered me in His presence. I found determination in trial, life in death, comfort in pain, healing in heartbreak, pride in guilt and remorse, purpose in affliction, integrity in desperation, and friendship in loneliness. I found God in faith.

Through interactions with family, friends, and colleagues, I found that many people struggle with the notion of prayer. You may be aware of the act of praying, but have you found yourself wondering about its purpose? Have you ever asked yourself: Why should I pray? Who do I pray to? How long should I pray for? What happens when I'm done praying? And where do I begin?

I found this to be a heartbreaking discovery, as prayer is one of the most important tools for living a prosperous, content life. Prayer is the bridge of communication linking people to Christ, and without prayer, we are left to live this life with no real, divine sense of direction. As a result of having no divine GPS, we look to other misled, confused people for a sense of direction.

Many of these "advisors" are confused about themselves, too. And how can they help us with our lives, if they cannot help themselves with their own lives?

Do you see the problem?

That's why I wrote this book.

Prayer has no time quota. Prayer is vulnerable. Prayer allows you to tell your truth to your Creator. Funnily enough, God already knows your truth. He just wants to feel it being breathed through the vessel He created: *you*. He is there to listen to you when no one else will...When no one else can.

My prayer is that you will understand the power acquired from being vulnerable with God. This is the purest form of power any person can possess, a power that is titillating above measure. This power grows deeper than the roots of the greatest black gum tree. This power relinquishes you from the chambers of your own heart.

Prayer is the vehicle that provides answers to your questions. Prayer is your blueprint and roadmap for life.

My hope is that, through reading the prayers in this book and seeing one's own vulnerability with God, you will learn *how* to approach God. You will realize just how efficacious prayer is. You will experience power through prayer. And you will live a more fulfilling life.

Prayer is not so much about creating change outside of you as it is about creating change on the inside of you.

Prayer changes lives for the better; I know it will change yours.

Enjoy the book, and enjoy praying.

God bless you,

A.J. Robert

Acknowledgments

To:

The Lord,
And every soul that played a role in His plan

Prayer 1

Dear Lord,

The sun rises, and then it sets. The pollen-filled flowers grow, bloom, and shortly thereafter, wither. Summers quickly turn to winters. Springs turn to falls. But Your love will always remain steadfast.

Thank you, Lord, for always loving me. There is no surreptitiousness to Your love. You do not hide it; it is exposed for all to see. Your love never fails, never dries, never comes to a halt.

Like a horse gallantly galloping down a path, Your love is rhythmic. Each step advancing in perfect harmony.

Your love is perfectly in tune with the timing my being loved necessitates.

Thank you, Lord.

Amen.

Prayer 2

Dear Father,

My obsequiousness grants me grace. I will wait, serving in Your presence forever. Lord, You are good all the time and I adore every precious facet of Yours. You can never be fully understood, but You leave enough crumbs for daily sustenance.

When I close my eyes, I see You. When I open my eyes, I feel You. When I shut my ears, I think of You. And when I close my mouth, I taste You. You provide for all my deepest, truest desires.

I will submit to Your reason for my existence, never knowing what will result from it in its entirety.

I trust You, more than I trust myself. You have never failed me in the previous; You must not fail me in the present.

Amen.

Prayer 3

Lord,

Some days I feel...lost. My soul longs for something, but nothing in particular. I am like a ship without a sail, tossing to and fro. Please change the course of the winds. Without hesitation, You must come to my rescue—in Your perfect timing.

When I am in imminent danger, You save me. When I am fond of depression, You guide me. When I am in my solitude, You tend to me.

Thank you for Your grace, mercy, and love.

Amen.

Prayer 4

Dear Father,

My fears b(l)inded me. My doubters shunned me. And scrutiny imprisoned me. Criticism was the warden.

I searched for love in deep, dark places, only to find that You have placed love in living.

Your love unveiled itself, freed me, and expunged my record.

Thank you, Lord.

Amen.

Prayer 5

Dear Lord,

My precociousness granted me wisdom, which simultaneously conceived sin. A natural desire for sin predated my knowledge of it. Time and again I give in to temptation. *Lust.* I love her, although she will never reciprocate. With her coy glances, she seduces me, but I know she will never love me. I still surrender to her every time.

Subsequently, shame closely trails behind. Like Adam and Eve, I hide—waiting, expecting to be quickly unveiled and chained. I sit and wallow in my pain. I painfully sit and wallow. I cry out. But then You help me realize that my sin is yet another reminder of Your perfection. You knew no sin, never succumbing to temptation.

You died for my sins so that I may have life, and have it more abundantly.

You freed me, unchaining me from my worldly pleasures. Laying my chains down, You prove to be love. And love liberates.

Thank you for loving me and then liberating me.

Amen.

Prayer 6

Dear Lord,

My sins bring me closer to You. Your grace rests at the crossroad between transgressions and repentance. You find me, even at the pinnacle of my pain. You do all things—except fail.

Amen.

Prayer 7

Dear Father,

I am defenseless against You. You formed me while I was still in my mother's womb. What's more, You had plans for me before I was even conceived. Because of this, I can lay my ambitions at Your feet, in submission to Your will.

I am submitted, Lord.

Amen.

Prayer 8

Lord,

When pathways present themselves, I look to You. I know that Your way is perfect. Your word says, "The steps of the righteous are ordered."[1] I can trust that nothing I have been through has been in vain. I can trust that everything I have experienced has prepared me for *this* moment—this moment right *here*.

Whitney Houston said it best when she said, "I look to you." I keep my eyes fixated on the hills. Please help me; please guide me. I know You hear me. You always hear me. You understand me even when I do not understand myself. I trust You.

I am imperfect. I am both yearning for and apprehensive about this next step. I know that You can—and You *will*—provide for me the discernment that I need.

Shift my mind, oh Lord. I will pay any price to grow closer to You. You are good and Your mercies are new each morning.

Thank you, Lord.

Amen.

Prayer 9

Dear Lord,

In the early of the morning, my lust clinches me. I try to turn my mind to everything else—*anything* else—but I am too weak. I stumble. I fall.

Your word says, "Though a righteous man falls, he will get up."[1] Your word says, "In my weakness, You are made strong."[2] Your word is what draws me back to my correct senses—my spiritual senses. The enemy attempts to lie to me, trampling me into states of depression and indecisiveness. But You bring clarity, oh Lord. You say You love me.

Thank you for Your word, which is the everlasting truth. Your word brings light to dark places, love to hateful places, enlightenment to ignorant places, and peace to strife-filled places.

Thank you that You are God.

Amen.

Prayer 10

Dear Lord,

The greatest thing about Your love is that I never deserve it. *Grace.* Your love never fails and always replenishes. Your love is a glorious refrain.

Amen.

Prayer 11

Dear Lord,

Even as a believer, I still fear. I still fear death. Your word says, "You did not instill in me the spirit of fear, but instead You instilled in me the spirits of power, love, and self-discipline."[1] This does not mean, though, that I will not experience fear.

I try to place my complete trust in You, but at times my efforts seem futile.

Help me, Lord. Help me to better put my complete trust in You. Show me, Lord. Show me Your unveiled power in my life. Help me to settle my soul.

Help me to exchange weakness for power, fear for love, and lusts for self-discipline.

Help me, Lord.

Amen.

Prayer 12

Dear Lord,

Just for today, please help me to *finish*.

Thank you.

Amen.

Prayer 13

Dear Lord,

Please grant me the nimbleness of mind to find discernment within my own indecisiveness. Please help me to walk in ways that are confident.

Amen.

Prayer 14

Dear Lord,

Thank you for the grace to serve. I am dust, whirling at Your will. Many are hurting, many are without, and many are in need, yet You have provided me with the ability to give. My dexterity in performing Your work speaks to Your omnipotence.

Thank you, Lord.

Amen.

Prayer 15

Dear Father,

Sometimes I let my ambition flood the streets where my desire for Your presence should meander. I let worldly cravings preface You. These wants never measure up to who You are. Wants never measure up to what You could be. At the satisfaction of these fits of hunger, I am left feeling emptier than before I had them.

Lord, teach me to value my days. Teach me to crave You. Teach me to not see our moments as mundane, but instead as monumental—never to be seen again.

Lord, I am menial, but You are magnificent. I will treat Your presence as such.

I will bless You, Lord. Thank you.

Amen.

Prayer 16

Lord,

There are moments when I struggle to read Your word. Yet, I will still trust in every proverb eloquently plotted on the pages. I will hold Your word near to my heart, letting nothing tear me and it apart. I will rest on its promises.

Please grant me sweet rest. My longing for rest established the most comfortable nest on sweet nectars dipped in pomegranates. Please grant me sweet, silky rest.

You are catered to my haste, never letting my mind waste.

Thank you, Lord.

Amen.

Prayer 17

Father Lord,

As I tired away, only one request remained: that Your gifts forever abound in my company. You never allow me to elude servitude.

Menial tasks appear mammoth. Sacrifice feels sublime. It all comes together, in the end, and in Your time.

Thank you, El Shaddai.

Amen.

Prayer 18

Dear Lord,

Good morning. Thank you for granting me another day. Not every man rises each day, but Your love rolls over like California hills. Your mercies are new each morning. Each daybreak is a new mercy, a fresh opportunity.

Amen.

Prayer 19

Lord,

I love to talk. Please help me to shut. my. mouth. Your word says, "The power of life and death lies in the tongue,"[1] and sometimes I let my tongue perform massacres. My tongue has killed relationships, dreams, opportunities, spirits, and—at times—me.

Please help me only to speak of love, grace, and truth. Help me to speak life into the dead and decaying. Help me to speak life into the proclamation of Your glory. Thank you for my tongue; please grant me the composure to control it.

Bless You, Lord.

Amen.

Prayer 20

Lord,

My sin straps me down. It places me on the offering table as I squirm, attempting to break free. Please free me. At times, my sins feel superior to me. They are too much to bear. They defeat me. Please place Your loving hands over me. Restore me.

Bring me into perfection with You. I do not want to sin. I do not want to live in opposition to Your will. My natural inclinations overwhelm me. I succumb to my own flesh.

My stresses ignite my vices, and my vices ignite my insecurities. My insecurities give birth to my sin, and my sin extinguishes my flame.

Set me ablaze, Lord. You are the refiner. Refine me, Lord. I beg You to rid me of all my impurities.

Help me, Lord.

Amen.

Prayer 21

Dear Lord,

Thank you for giving me the opportunity to experience another day, another chance to breathe. I thank You that You are full of mercy—I always need mercy. You have forgiven me over and over again, and for that, I am at Your service.

My appetite for sin is never satisfied. I always want more. My thirst is insatiable. This world provides a myriad of avenues to conceive sin, and I know each and every one of them. Lord, please help me to vanquish my dark side, which is a side that knows no boundaries.

When I feel depleted, I am reminded that Your word says, "My grace is sufficient for you."[1] And I praise You for Your sufficiency of grace. You are worthy of all praise. You are worthy of all honor.

I praise You, Lord.

Amen.

Prayer 22

Lord,

Please bless my life. I have new desires, passions, business endeavors, and burnings for intimacy. I pray that each longing is in alignment with Your will. Your word says, "I will give you your heart's desires."[1] I pray that my desires are established by You and not by my own ambition—which will likely be the death of me.

I pray that I may walk in Your footsteps and integrity, and that I am saturated in Your word. Lord, lead my mind; Lord, lead my life. You are the purifier of my soul and I bow down low in Your presence.

Thank you, Lord.

Amen.

Prayer 23

Dear Lord,

Please help me to subdue yesterday's antagonist. He is constantly attempting to resurrect himself. He is toxic, and so is the company he keeps. They care nothing about me, and they care nothing about themselves. Knowing they are doomed, they belch seductive echoes to pull as many people down to the graves as possible.

These gargoyles have no place in my life, but they yearn for one desperately. They yearn for many.

Your word says that I must "take off the old man and put on the new man."[1]

Please clothe me in this dignified tapestry that is purposed to elevate me. Please clothe me in integrity.

Vestiges of the old man must be completely auctioned off.

Please help me, Lord.

Amen.

Prayer 24

Dear Lord,

Paul speaks of having a "thorn" in his flesh.[1] He describes this thorn to be a messenger from Satan, sent to keep him from becoming proud. Some people assume this thorn was a malady or illness. Others think Paul's thorn was blindness or visual impairment. I presume Paul battled lust.

For a man of God who appears to have much of his life in order, lust is a crippling enemy. It is an embarrassing struggle: how can a man perform miracles, yet not be able to control his own genitalia's desires?

Lust hates its enemies, and lust is a powerful beast. I am convinced lust cannot ever be leashed. Instead, lust puts *its* foes on a leash, and when they believe that they are finally free, lust cuts the slack, reminding them that they are forever bound.

If all this is the truth, then I am like Paul who mismanaged his craving. The *self* can be the most difficult to manage. Lord, please help me to manage myself.

Thank you, Lord.

Amen.

Prayer 25

Dear Lord,

I hear "move," but I feel afraid. I hear "move," but I look at my finances. I hear "move," but I hear what my family says. I hear "move," but I look at my job situation. I hear "move," but I look at my expenses. I hear "move," but I see educational opportunities.

Where do I go? Which way do I turn? When will I know? I hear You say, "The anointing is not on the place; the anointing is on you. I will provide for you, wherever you go."[1] I will trust in You, Lord. I will submit to Your ways.

Perhaps the enemy and temptation are after me so much because they know that my recent graduation was an impetus for graduating in many other areas in my life. The enemy does not want me to do more Kingdom work. As long as I remain in my small pond, I will produce small results. The enemy does not mind smallness. It is my *growth* that the enemy hates. The enemy fears Kingdom expansion.

Please give me confirmation, Lord. Divulge unto me the obvious message.

Thank you, Father.

Amen.

Prayer 26

Dear Lord,

Thank you for another opportunity to experience Your daylight. Today, I have nothing in particular to pray for, yet I know that I must pray. Thank you that Your word says, "When I don't know what I ought to pray for, the Holy Spirit intercedes for me, interpreting my groaning."[1] Today, Lord, I groan for You. You know my thoughts, Lord.

I will serve You all of my days.

Amen.

Prayer 27

Dear Lord,

Please help me to control my emotions. Some days my responses are more quick-witted and short-fused than others. My emotions attempt to control, and in the heat of the moment, they feel right. It seems as if they have my best interests at heart. But I know this is not always true.

Emotions are finicky. They lie. They are selfish. And they can easily be manipulated. Emotions are perfidious and cannot be trusted. Emotions are promiscuous, catering to anything that coddles them.

Lord, please help me to hold my emotions at bay.

Amen.

Prayer 28

Dear Lord,

I was a victim. I *am* a victim. I am a victim of the brutality of being unloved. My own contemplated aborting me, and another aborted me before they even knew they conceived me. Being unloved, when fully grown, matured to manipulation. Lord, I just wanted someone to love me. I wanted someone to hold me and tell me that everything would be alright. I wanted the void filled. I wanted to feel the truest warmth of another being—a warmth only the soul can detect as true. I knew I was raised deprived of human interaction, but I never understood how this deprivation might affect my childhood, my adulthood, and by extension, my entire life.

I often gave everything You blessed me with. And for what? A short time with a person who, without hesitation, would have aborted me too? Lord, please forgive me. For I never knew I was covetous for You. The grandeur of Your word and love evaporated every longing I had for human acceptance. Your word is efficacious: "Whom the Son set free is truly free indeed."[1]

Thank you, Lord. You set me free. You truly set me free from myself.

Amen.

Prayer 29

Lord,

This is the day that You have made; I will rejoice and be glad in it. Today is a very good day—a special day.

This day is yet another reminder that I do not need the accolades. I do not need my name in glaring lights. I only need You.

You have claimed victory. Nothing can limit You. I must not put anything before You. I must not put anything above You.

I lay my all at Your throne. Thank you for the love that You have shown.

I will serve You every day.

Merci Seigneur,

Amen

Prayer 30

Lord,

Please help me to be stable. I know I must stay humble. You are God, and my place to You is nothing but dust.

Lord, the enemy comes to steal, kill, and destroy. And he wants me to be his subject. On all sides, I am attacked. But on all sides, You are also with me.

Lord, I look to You. I look to You in every trial of my life.

Amen.

Prayer 31

Lord,

Please help me to not place love itself on the throne. I do not want to crave anything more than I crave You. Your word says, "For what does it profit a man to gain the whole world but lose his soul?"[1] I have everything. I must first be faithful over little things before You can trust me with great things.

If I am honest with myself, I do not deserve more.

I do not deserve life.

My faith is little. My addictions are many. My mind is tainted. My work ethic is poor. My grudges are strong. My jealousy is relentless. My animosity is efficacious.

I would have left me years ago. Yet, Your grace remains.

Good thing I am not You.

Thank you, Lord.

Amen.

Prayer 32

Good morning Lord,

Thank you for granting me peaceful rest. I am floating in Your green pastures and I must not take for granted the serenity of its stillness.

I appreciate the blessings You have showered upon me. You have shown me, throughout my life, that Your love for me has always been consistent—from trial to triumph.

Sometimes everyday moments morph into the mundane—and I miss Your presence. But when I peer through the rear-view mirror of my life, I realize that every moment was a miracle.

Every moment was a lavishing of Your goodness and sovereignty.

Every moment was an unction.

Thank you, Lord, for Your presence.

Amen.

Prayer 33

Dear Lord,

I allow many distractions to infiltrate my mind daily. I do not know how to keep my mind centered on You and Your purpose for my life. In these moments, I feel weak. I want answers from You but I have no motivation to take to my knees, close my eyes, and pursue You. Please help resuscitate my need for You.

It is in my need that I aggregate ambition. This is a dangerous prayer; I am fearful of how You will answer this prayer as I pray it, yet I am certain that You always have my best interest at heart.

There are moments in my prayers when I do not know what to say; You still understand me. There are moments in my life when I do not know what to do; You still guide me. Your word says, "You lead me beside peaceful streams and You restore my soul."[1]

Please restore my soul, Lord.

Thank you.

Amen.

Prayer 34

Dear Lord,

You are faithful. You continually seek me in the midnight hours, when You know I am most available. You attempt to talk to me throughout the day, but I am oblivious to Your voices.

I cast You off to the side. I marginalize You. For this, I sincerely apologize.

When I languish in my iniquities, You diligently and faithfully remind me of Your presence.

In my melancholic moments, Your love falls upon me like the most tempestuous of cascades, and my trepidations vanish.

I marvel at the immensity of Your power, Lord.

I love You.

Amen.

Prayer 35

Dear Lord,

Today I faced rejection. They cut me off so quickly. It hurts to face rejection over and over again. Why do You make suggestions only for me to be let down? What do You want me to learn from these disappointments? Will these disappointments make the actual attainment more enjoyable? Am I learning to appreciate and cherish the blessing that is to come because of the disappointments I faced along the way? Maybe that's it.

Or maybe I should learn to appreciate what I already have, that which truly does love me, and that which asks for nothing in return. I swear I am doing what You ask of me, yet I keep hitting brick walls. Disappointments dismay me; I am tired. What should I be doing? When should I be doing it? Where should I be doing it? Who should I be doing it with?

Yet, I will still choose to rejoice in rejection. Your word says, "They went out from us, but they did not really belong to us. For if they had belonged to us, they would have remained with us; but their going showed that none of them belonged to us."[1] And that girl was not mine. What's mine will prove itself. It will love me, as I love it. It will love me when I do not show love to it—like You always do.

I know You are the epitome of true love. I will delight in You.

Thank you for Your many lessons, Lord. I am learning.

Amen.

Prayer 36

Dear Lord,

You are the shelter in the storm. For many, the darkness is the shadow of death; for Your people, the shadow is just shade. You give rest in the shade of Your wings.

Lead me, every moment of my life. I do not know what I would do without You. I cannot—I *do* not—want to even imagine a life separated from You.

Thank you, God.

Amen

Prayer 37

Dear Lord,

Why are You silent? Am I on the right track? Are You waiting for me to make the next move? Do You care? Where are You?

I am reminded of Your word that says, "When you seek me wholeheartedly, you will find me."[1]

Am I the one who has been silent, Lord? Have You been trying to speak to me all along, but have I allowed the business (and busyness) of this life to suffocate our communication channel? Am I the problem, Lord?

Lord, my prayers begin to feel decrepit. I have no recollection of when this first began. Reading Your word feels as if it has lost its vigor. How can I replenish our communication, Lord?

How can I make our dialogue glow like honey-auburn stars? What can I do to make us rich?

I pray, I read, and I write; yet, I am still stale. I am lukewarm, and I know it. Lord, help me to do what I need to. Please walk me closer to You.

Thank you, Father.

Amen

Prayer 38

Dear Lord,

I sinned...again. I am aware of Your mercy, but I am still grieved with guilt. Please rid me of this sin. Help me to tame myself.

I no longer want to be a slave to sin, bereft of self-control. Instead, I want to be cleansed of all evil.

Permeate purity throughout my existence.

Your word says, "For God was in Christ, reconciling the world to himself, no longer counting people's sins against them. And He gave us this wonderful message of reconciliation."[1]

I believe Your word. I will rebuttal my evilness, using Your word.

Your word always wins.

Thank you, Lord.

Amen.

Prayer 39

Lord,

Please help me. In my life, I pursue many endeavors. My hope is that they are all according to Your will. I do not want to take a single step unaligned with Your path.

You are a merciful God, but You are also a loving Father. And sometimes fathers allow their children to go off course for the sole purpose of allowing a glorious return to propriety. I never want to be off-kilter.

Lord, speak to me; speak to my heart.

Let me feel Your presence.

Speak to me in ways that I have never experienced. Make Yourself known. Reveal Yourself to me. I love You, Lord.

Thank you.

Amen.

Prayer 40

For You, Father,

Kiss me, oh Lord, and show me Your ways. Guide me, oh Lord, and lead me each day.

Coronate me with the splendor of Your magnificence. Let Your glory be a reverberation in my life, seeping into every crevice of my being.

Show me where You are, and I will make that place my home. These streets abhor the Godly, rendering them unsafe for anyone to roam.

Be a lamp to guide my feet, a cushion for me to rest, and a wholesome meal to eat.

Kiss me, oh Lord, and show me Your ways.

Guide me, oh Lord, and lead me each day.

Coronate me with the splendor of Your magnificence.

Amen.

Prayer 41

Lord,

In the midnight hour, I will seek Your presence. I will seek Your face. I come before You thanking You for You. You have shown me an abundance of love. I cannot thank You enough. You have shielded me from death. You have made me impervious to threats, hostilities, snide comments, and disdain.

I am under the protection of Your wings.

The enemy that I now face is myself. The enemy attempts to mislead my thinking. When You will not allow the devil to touch me, he blows hateful kisses from afar. He hates me, yet he conceals his hate in falsified love.

You are my strength.

I pray to You, Lord, and only You. Thank you for life. It is Your method of revealing love. I will always remain oblivious to just how deeply Your love seeps.

Thank you, Lord.

Amen.

Prayer 42

Dear Lord,

I know this is a dangerous prayer to pray, but please help me with my patience. I feel that it has run entirely dry. I have none left to give.

Amen.

Prayer 43

Dear Lord,

Today I pray to You frustrated. I always desire to be busy, but I do not know what I should do. What steps should I take? When should I start? Who should I speak with first?

I am always *going*.

I don't even know where to. I guess I just want more. But the more I chase, the more I achieve; the more I achieve, the emptier I become.

Worldly accomplishments do not give me what I truly, deeply long for. Every achievement is a more vivid depiction of how only You have the ability to satisfy.

Only You can satisfy my heart. Only You can quench my thirst.

Quell my longings, Lord.

Reprimand my greed.

Amen.

Prayer 44

Dear Lord,

Thank You for giving me another sunrise to watch. Your existence is known through Your creations. There was a beginning, and I refuse to believe molecules appeared out of nowhere, collided, and created an entire space system composed of smaller planetary systems.

I refuse to believe that You do not exist. Lord, there are moments when I have disbelief. Like Thomas, I have tendencies to doubt. But, like Moses, I go anyway. I am thankful that You are patient with me. When I don't know, You speak my language. And when I do know, You reveal even more to me —unveiling more of my ignorance.

You show me, Lord, that believing in You takes faith. Lord, Your word says, "Blessed are those who have not seen You."[1] My faith is real. It is irrevocable. Trials will come, but I believe that, without faith, life is not worth living. You gave the world around me to serve as a memento of Your existence. In every season, I will turn my eyes to the hills.

I will bless You, Lord. Thank you.

Amen.

Prayer 45

Dear Lord,

There are many days when I do not feel beautiful. I am constantly comparing myself to others, examining what they have, and pouting over that which I do not. I am insecure. I want more. I desire more. I allow my wants to overshadow my possessions. I am often ungrateful for what You have already provided for me. And I am on the verge of collapse. How can I be thankful for my current situation? How can I be grateful for my *now*? What can I turn to, to understand the full magnitude of my life? Where can I find appreciation?

My feelings of inadequacy cage me in obscurity, where darkness falls upon me like twilight. Night after night, I am lulled to sleep by ignorance. I abhor this sickness that consistently robs me of my present. Where is Your safe haven, Lord? I am in dire need of You. Where can I go to escape this duress?

Well, Lord, I pour my entire heart out to You. I cannot give my heart to anything else. Nothing else will cherish it the way that You do. You have an affinity for me; You truly care for me. Your love is an anomaly: something I have never—and *will* never—experience from another being.

I believe Your word.

You keep on loving me.

Thank you, Lord.

A.J. ROBERT

Amen.

Prayer 46

Dear Lord,

I am weary. Work has worn me down today. Please give me the strength I need to make it through the day. Please help me to keep my soul grounded in patience, my attitude positioned in love, and my mind focused on Your word.

Make me aware of my actions. I do not intend to give birth to damage from my own frustrated state of mind. Only You can create in me pure motives and actions.

I will be rectified in You.

Thank you, Lord.

Amen.

Prayer 47

Dear Lord,

When it is cold, You are my warmth. Your radiant beams stir glory within my soul. It is an honor to serve You, to have a loving God who always extends His receptor without conniption. You reprimand with loving-kindness.

Your way is always good—an anomaly. I will be cleansed like ivory. And one day, I will be brought into perfect peace with You.

Lord, You are the author of my life, and I will submit to Your plan for my being.

Lead me, Lord.

Amen.

Prayer 48

Dear Lord,

Please show me what I am holding onto that I must give away. Actually, I know what it is. You have answered my prayer before I can even finish praying it.

Thank you, Lord.

Amen.

Prayer 49

Dear Lord,

Today, I feel like I am falling again. I am like a toddler stumbling over his own uncoordinated, clanky feet. I am pressed between the same old, previous lifestyles of my yesterdays. I have a litany of addictions; which one should I indulge today? I drink from rancid pools of water, desperately attempting to nourish myself.

Help me to subdue my self-demeaning behavior. Why must I go through this? Why is this problem gripping me? I did not choose it; it chose me.

Help me, Lord. Please free me.

Amen.

Prayer 50

Dear Lord,

I pray my mouth does not write me tickets my future does not want to pay for. Please help me to keep my composure. Your word says, "Whoever guards his mouth preserves his life; he who opens wide his lips comes to ruin."[1]

I do not want to be a hydrant, spewing hate, malice, and contention in every direction. I want to speak truthfully, gracefully; I want to deliver and assert with care.

Only with Your guidance can I truly achieve these desires. Only through Your power can I truly become all that You have planned for me to become.

Lord, I look to You for guidance in every area of my life. I cannot come to You only for healing or affluence.

I must come to You for mediation in my family matters, work matters, mental matters...every matter.

I love You, Lord.

Amen.

Prayer 51

Dear Lord,

What is next? I have a hearing issue. I cannot hear You. I want what You want, but I am a hypocrite. I do not pray, not nearly enough.

I see Your word. But I do not understand it. It is a foreign language to me. I am afraid only the fire can change me. Change me, oh God. Make me over again.

I have a host of habits, and I do not know how to evict them. Be the bailiff, Lord. Create in me something new.

Cure me. Cure my senses, Lord. Inoculate me, Father.

I am desperate for You, Lord. I will forever worship You, pursuing You with complete optimism and love.

Thank you, God.

Amen.

Prayer 52

Dear Lord,

Thank you for this day. You have blessed me tremendously, and for that, I am forever indebted to You. You have been my protector, provider, and shelterer in every season of my life.

You were alongside me before I even knew who I was.

You give grace and mercy. When I do not deserve Your love, You give me an extra portion.

Thank you for this day, Lord. Thank you that You are love.

Amen.

Prayer 53

Dear Lord,

My prayer life is beginning to fade away. Please give me the strength and desire to continually seek Your presence. I cannot let the circumstances of this world overshadow my need for You.

Without You, I am nothing. Without You, I cannot be. Without You, my existence is purposeless. Please help me, Lord, to always see that I need You in every moment, event, and season of my life. My seeking of You can never become trite.

Thank you, Lord, that You are good.

Amen.

Prayer 54

Dear Lord,

Please grant me patience today. I am stretched, spread thin and wide over a surface of discomfort. I am tired of people. I long for more. I am in desperate anticipation of the next breakthrough in my life. I know I will have to face new challenges, but I believe I am prepared. My current challenges have become mundane, and there are few things worse than an old challenge.

Please push me forward, Lord.

I love You.

Thank you, God.

Amen.

Prayer 55

Dear Lord,

Thank you for giving me the grace to perform my job. I am great at what I do, and I know it is only because of You. You supply intellect. You have given me intelligence, wit, and expediency beyond my own capacity.

Lord, please continue to hold my hand.

Thank you, Lord.

Amen.

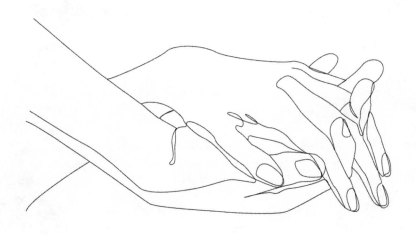

Prayer 56

Dear God,

I am in a moment of utter and complete dissatisfaction with life. Nothing seems to satisfy. I am guilt-ridden, shame-filled, lonely, tired, and pressed on all sides. My day has turned gloomy. Optimism has vacated the premises. Frustration has started a riot. Yet, I remain stoic.

How do I rebuttal moments such as this one? How do I evade my own misery? Where can I turn? Where can I hide?

No ocean shore can divert my attention. No summer breeze can redirect my focus. No rain shower can still my soul. I am beaten up, bruised, and abused.

What is temporary will have been temporary. What is eternal will last. When my light goes out, my hope is to be postured resolute in Your presence.

My moral is meager, sustaining my humility. Thank you, Lord, for this thorn.

Goodnight, Father.

Amen.

Prayer 57

Dear Lord,

Today has been a very difficult day for me. I feel as if I am in a waiting room, and have been for years. Please forgive me for my unwillingness to wait. I rush. I am impatient.

I know that many are in worse conditions than me, yet I still choose to focus only on myself. I am selfish. I have not even begun to give thought to others' conditions. I can be self-centered.

Lord, please show me Your ways. Please show me how to have more patience.

How can I learn such a thing?

I will do my best to continue to wait on You and serve while I wait.

Thank you.

Amen.

Prayer 58

Dear Lord,

Thank you for this day. Today was completely and utterly beautiful. I spent the day entirely with You, abiding in Your presence. Your glory is amazing when I am caught in worship. Your aura is captivating. There is no other place I would rather be.

Thank you, God.

Amen.

Prayer 59

Dear God,

Thank you for blessing me with another day. You have kept me humble. You never allow me to become too proud of my accomplishments, for these accomplishments are not my own. I am simply a vessel, a shell through which Your purpose can be fulfilled here on earth.

I must never become arrogant. *You* are my leader. *You* are my reason. I want You and only You.

Thank you, God.

Amen.

Prayer 60

Dear Lord,

You have blessed me immensely. I do not deserve Your gifts. Why do You give them? It is because You love me; it must be. Your undeserved gifts are a graphic depiction of grace.

I promise You, Lord. I vow to never let this beautiful woman become the epicenter of us. I love her so much, but I love You more.

She is everything I ever dreamed of—and more. Her skin glows like an aircraft piercing through the clouds into the brilliant sunlight. Her teeth are perfectly aligned. Her cheeks are perfectly pooled of purity. She is silly and laughs at her own jokes.

Her happiness makes me happy. Her skin is smooth and she smells of pure, fresh cocoa butter. I did not have to change who I was for her to love me.

As I became more like You, her love for me grew higher, deeper, wider.

I want to protect her. I want to give her everything I have. I want to serve her. Why did You give her to me without warning? She arrived so fast. I thought this gift was taking forever, but when she arrived, she arrived in a heartbeat.

Love is fast and it does not knock on the door. Love comes without warning, without invitation, and without hesitation. Love is light and airy.

This is an amazing love story, and I know it is only the beginning. She and I have distance to cover, education to attain, finances to fund, sights to behold, cuisines to indulge in, egos to overcome, spirits to sacrifice, naysayers to ignore, children to birth, a church to lead, a world to change, a life to live, and a God to serve—You.

Thank you, Lord. She is beautiful. But of course, she would be; she came from You.

You are amazing,

Amen.

Prayer 61

Dear Lord,

Today has stretched me. My patience has been pressed. How can I remain humble yet assertive? How can I hear You more clearly? How can I remain in Your presence? I only want to hear You.

I do not want any other voices to influence me.

You are the best advisor. I only want to commune with You.

Thank you, Lord.

Amen.

Prayer 62

Dear Lord,

I am already beginning to feel my attention shifting. My mind is constantly thinking about her. I love her but I will never allow her to become my God like You are.

Please help me to keep focus. Please remind me that only You can love me the way I need to be loved.

I also pray for protection and direction over her and her family. Please guide them in their difficult time.

I trust You, and I love You.

Amen.

Prayer 63

Dear Lord,

Thank you for blessing me. Your blessings are as numerous and extravagant as the constellations above the earth. I will always praise Your name. Lord, please continue to bless me and expand my territory, and give me neither pain nor suffering.

You are my God and I will never fear what comes my way. Your word says that You did not give us (people) the spirit of fear, but instead, You instilled in us the spirits of *power, love,* and *self-discipline.* I will put my trust and hope and faith in You—and You alone.

I know I will be tested. I trust You to be at my side.

Goodnight, Lord.

I love You.

Amen.

Prayer 64

Dear Lord,

Please help me. My enemies outnumber me and surround me on every side. They smile in my face, as if I am not aware that they are planning wickedness against me. They devise schemes. And they do wrong. Then they search for an innocent bystander to throw under the bus. They attempt to asphyxiate me, not knowing You are my source of oxygen.

Your word says, "If God be for me, who can be against me?"[1] Your word says, "No weapon formed against me shall prosper."[2] I will trust Your word. I know I can lean on You in times of trouble.

I will not be afraid. I will listen and wait for Your instruction. You see every plot from far off, before it even reaches me.

Teach me to be ambidextrous in life, Lord. Teach me to fend off enemies while nourishing myself. You "preparest a table before me in the presence of my enemies."[3] Teach me how to ignore them while I eat.

Thank you, Lord.

Amen.

Prayer 65

Dear Lord,

Thank you for waking me up this morning. I am so thankful to have another chance at life. My existence is proof that You have more to give: You have more to *give* to me and more to *do* through me.

Thank you for keeping me humble. I want to constantly seek humility so that You never have to humble me. I fear You, God. I've seen the smallest fraction of what You can do.

Lord, please remain first in every area of my life.

I love You.

Amen.

Prayer 66

Dear Lord,

I worship You. I often come to You, pleading for You to fulfill my every desire. Today will be different. I will come before You, humbly serving You. You are God and there is none other like You.

Nothing can compare to Your magnificence, and my frailty gives reason to why I praise Your Glory.

In all of Your glory, You have managed to make me—little *me*—an heir.

The fullness of Your blessings makes the richest places on earth appear desolate—penniless.

Create in me a longing, a fire for You that can only be quenched by You.

I love You, God.

Amen.

Prayer 67

Dear Lord,

I am in the valley of the shadow of death. I trust You to protect me.

Amen.

Prayer 68

Dear Lord,

I am surrounded by wolves on every side. They are filled with so much hate that they begin to attack each other. They do not realize their own savagery. At times, I do not realize my own savagery either.

Please help them. Please help me. Help us to realize the moments when hate, selfishness, and pride have erected.

In these moments, I hear You say:

"Blessed are the poor in spirit, for theirs is the Kingdom of Heaven. Blessed are those who mourn, for they will be comforted. Blessed are the meek, for they will inherit the earth. Blessed are those who hunger and thirst for righteousness, for they will be filled. Blessed are the merciful, for they will be shown mercy. Blessed are the pure in heart, for they will see God. Blessed are the peacemakers, for they will be called children of God. Blessed are those who are persecuted because of righteousness, for theirs is the kingdom of heaven."[1]

Thank you, Lord.

Amen.

Prayer 69

Dear Lord,

Thank you for this day. It is one that You have made. I will rejoice and be glad in it.

Please give me the discernment and wisdom I need to manage my emotions and the emotions of others.

Amen.

Prayer 70

Dear Lord,

I pray for a peaceful night's rest. Please help me to sleep soundly tonight. May I bask in Your bountiful presence forever and ever.

Thank you for my life; it is a blessing to be alive and to live.

Lord, thank you for being my God. You are magnificent beyond my comprehension. Without You, I don't know where I would be. There is no way that I would be able to survive without Your presence in my life. I would have committed spiritual suicide.

You granted me so many blessings—more than I can carry, more than I can manage.

You have kept me protected in the storm. You have kept me sheltered during the rain. You provided a boat for me in the tumultuous seas.

Thank you, Lord. I love You.

Amen.

Prayer 71

Dear Lord,

Today I need You more than ever. This spiritual warfare is nothing like I have seen before; it is more dangerous. I have had visions of prisons, disasters, atrocities, death, and blood. Lord, please surround me with Your angels. Please grant me peace of mind so that I may be able to do Your work and do it successfully.

Thank you, Lord, for giving me the opportunity to see today's sunlight. Thank you for giving me the opportunity to wake up once more. I surely will not take this for granted.

Please detox my mind, Lord. I know that the battle I am facing is not of flesh and blood, but instead, it is a spiritual battle. This battle is against principalities and spirits of the dark world.

Please help me to see You in the midst. Please strengthen me, Lord. I will do my best to serve You and to serve You righteously. Please help me to see the purpose behind these visions, Lord, and help me to preach Your word with both courage and humility, and with grace and truth.

Thank you, Lord.

Amen.

Prayer 72

Dear Lord,

The soil for ministry is fertile. Please help me to develop the strength that I will need to preach to a congregation—a people that are hurting, tired, and in need of a savior. Today, I awoke pressed beyond measure, like Paul. Today, I awoke with a mind that felt deprived. I did not have the energy necessary to lead any sheep toward You. Today, I will do my best to serve You in the capacity that my gifts will allow me.

Lord, please stand alongside me as I look to You and point others to You as the source of all strength. Thank you, Lord. You are always continuing to bless me. Thank you, Lord, for speaking to my soul in ways that my mind can never comprehend.

Thank you, Lord, for always revealing Your grace, love, and compassion in the tiniest things in life.

Lord, I pray that this day will be fruitful. I pray that this day will not only be a blessing to me, but to those that come into contact with me.

Thank you, Lord.

Amen.

Prayer 73

Dear Lord,

I often struggle to show the world who I am; I often struggle to show the world *me*. Please, Lord. Please give me the strength to accept who I am, to accept who I could be, and to accept who I want to be.

I want to be made in Your image: I want to be made more whole and more perfected. Lord, relationships in love have shown me that I need to be honest about who I am. If I am not honest about who I am, I cannot receive the most honest form of love. Because showing who I truly am gives people the opportunity to love the real me. I have learned how to disguise myself.

I have learned how to camouflage myself. I have learned how to project a false identity. And, as a result, I have deprived myself of true love.

I have hidden from myself.

Lord, please teach me and give me the strength to project the truth so that I can be loved truthfully and purely.

Amen.

Prayer 74

Dear Lord,

Anxiety and nervousness are attempting to weigh me down. My expectations are high. My spirits are low. But I will turn to You as my source of strength. I will turn to You as my source of stability. Lord, devour this dubious spirit. Upheave this mentality of inadequacy.

Consume my mind. Console my heart. Control my spirit. Lead me beside the peaceful streams. Make me rest in green meadows. Prepare a table before me in the presence of my enemies and then give me the strength and the confidence to enjoy the meal.

Lord, You have been so good to me, but sometimes my eyesight needs a little bit of adjusting. Be my optometrist. Be my doctor. Help me to see the truth, to accept the truth, and to be set free by the truth.

Thank you, Lord.

Amen.

Prayer 75

Dear Lord,

You have put the perfect words in my mouth, once again. Your power amazes me. You create divine intervention; You *are* divine intervention. When I feel ill-prepared, You show me that You can step in at any time and project a masterpiece. I am in awe of You.

Please continue to provide me with the grace that I will need to fulfill Your mission and Your purpose here on Earth.

My feeble mind will never be able to fully comprehend the extent of Your omnipotence. My meager understanding can never comprehend You. I hope that my words transform the lives of Your people and the lives of all who hear them. I know that my time here is finite. I just hope that I create the change required of me. I hope that I can enjoy more beauties of life. I will do my best to serve You until my clock expires. I look forward to marriage. I look forward to a thriving relationship. I look forward to children. I look forward to grandchildren. I look forward to retirement. I look forward to You.

Lord, please continue to be with me, and please continue to be by my side. I love You with all that I have and with all that I am, and I pray that my actions will always please You.

Thank you, Lord.

Amen.

Prayer 76

Dear Lord,

I know that these urges are stress-induced, but I have to be honest with myself. When I ask for new endeavors, when I ask for new beginnings, I must also be ready and willing to handle the pressure. I asked for transformation. I asked for change. I asked for this. Now I am begging You for the strength, the courage, the patience, and the peace to continue to move forward.

Lord, thank you for answering my previous prayers. Please answer my present prayers. I know that I can trust You. Lord, I know that everything that I will need will be supplied. Yes, I will have to do some work, but You are also Jehovah-Jireh, my provider.

Thank you, Lord. Thank you, Lord. Thank you, Lord. Please continue to guide me. Please continue to stand by me in every area that You send me to.I feel the pressure, but I know You can relieve it as well. Please give me the wisdom and discernment I need to not redirect my pressures and stresses into an unhealthy lifestyle.

Please place the proper individuals in my life—and at the right time—to give me the proper advice that I need in every single moment. Lord, thank you. Father, I am humbled by this opportunity. I can be thankful for every opportunity, but every opportunity also requires a new version of me, a version of me that must be stronger than the last version. I have to be willing to stand strong, stand higher, and stand firmer. Thank you, Lord.

In Jesus's name, I pray.

Amen.

Prayer 77

Dear Lord,

Today, I need You desperately. You are the ultimate counselor, and I need Your wisdom. Guide me in my decision-making, and lead me down the proper path. Without Your guidance, I will continually make bad decisions. Only Your wisdom can successfully navigate me through the rubble of strife.

Please, Lord. Hold my hand and guide me every step of the way.

Amen.

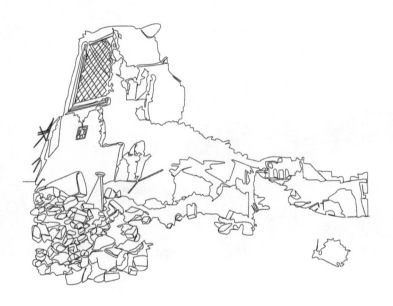

Prayer 78

Dear Lord,

Please continue to protect me. Things are changing. Life is new. Fear is in the air. But I know You are there as well. Please continue to be in the midst. Please continue to show Your power. Please continue to protect. You are all-powerful, and what You say will be.

I submit this prayer in Jesus's name.

Amen.

Prayer 79

Dear Lord,

Thank you for this day. Your mercies are new every morning, and I am very grateful that they are.

As much as I love You, as much as I surrender to You, as much as I glorify You, as much as I submit to You, I still am not impervious to my human inclinations.

Break me down gracefully. And make me stronger in Your refinement. I do not want to shame You, nor do I want to disobey You. Lord, perfection is impossible for me on this side of the dirt. But I ask that You continue to give me strength in every area of my life.

It is proven that I am human, and I often do what my flesh desires. Please continue to pour into me. Please continue to stir in me a willingness, a deep desire, to do right.

I love You, Lord, and I desire to be just a little bit closer to You.

Amen.

Prayer 80

Dear Lord,

Please take away the stress that I currently feel. My stress derives from a desire to be perfect, but I know I will never be perfect. Lord, I need You in every single moment of my life. I want to be the best that I can be for every single person that I encounter. I want to love without barriers. I want patience without pride. I want peace without strife. I want grace and truth.

Lord, thank you for the many blessings that You have bestowed upon me. There is no way that I can never repay You. I will do everything in my power to show You how much I appreciate You.

Lord, please continue to keep me sheltered and protected. Please keep Your hand of protection over me as I walk through this valley of the shadow of death. I know my health is not my own. You covered me this far, and I know what You will continue to cover me.

Thank you, Lord.

Amen.

Prayer 81

Dear Lord,

Temptation is crouching at the door, eager to dethrone Your children. Opportunities to sin are everywhere. Temptation wants to discredit Your people.

But we will stand firm. *I* will stand firm. I will remember Your teachings. I will gird myself with Your armor. Your word says, "Put on the whole armor of God so that I may be able to stand against the wiles of the devil."[1]

The enemy wants my mind. He wants all of my senses. If he can thwart what I sense, he can thwart what I believe.

But I will shun the devil.

I will not allow myself to be overcome by his wickedness.

Lord, You are my strength and my redeemer. I will run to You every. single. time.

Lord, please be with me.

Amen.

Prayer 82

Dear Lord,

Thank you for giving me strength on a daily basis. Without Your daily strength and guidance, my decisions are impetuous and elementary. You give provisions to combat my inhibitions. You meet me where I am and You do not shame me.

My words, hailing Your glory, will always be inadequate. But I will forever bow in Your presence.

You are a deliverer, and You deliver Your people from the hands of their enemies.

You even deliver Your people from themselves.

Thank you for never abandoning me; I have given You reason to many times.

Thank you, Lord,

Amen.

Prayer 83

Dear Lord,

I need You in every area of my life. I am fighting an enemy I cannot see, and I need You to be my eyes, ears, and hands. Please guide my efforts. Always inform my actions.

This battle, I cannot even begin to fight. I am up against a giant that towers over me.

But I will not be discouraged. Instead, I will turn to You with every ounce of hope I have. You are there. You are *here*.

I know that my life is not my own. It is a gift. You gifted me with this. I owe it completely and entirely to You.

I must not be stingy with a life that does not even belong to me. I need only Your power and authority.

Lord, please cover me and grant me more. Please walk alongside me with every endeavor. Please, Lord, shield me from every problem and all agony.

I will walk with You, Lord.

Amen.

Prayer 84

Dear Lord,

I am unworthy of every blessing You have ever bestowed upon me. I am unworthy of living. Lord, my biggest fears are mishandling and fumbling Your blessings.

I am not asking to be perfect, but I deeply desire to be close to it. I know failure is part of life and is thus inevitable in some areas.

There are other areas of my life where I cannot afford to make a mistake.

I want to be perfect in Your eyes. And if I am perfect in Your eyes, then no man can find fault with me.

I want to love You, love my wife, love my family, love my church, and love Your people.

Please grant me the wisdom, patience, emotional fortitude, and nimbleness of mind to hold fast to You.

You are omnipotent, Lord.

Amen.

Prayer 85

Dear Lord,

Thank you for another day. You are gracious and merciful. You grant me that which I do not even deserve. You have sheltered my entire family. You have provided a shady place for me to rest.

I must admit, life gets tiring. I am stretched. Oftentimes, I believe I am stretched beyond my own capacity. I am tested, daily. I am tried, consistently. I am pressed, constantly. But I will not give up. Even in my sin, I will not faint. I will close my ears and eyes to my rivalries of this world. I will prevail.

Your word says, "Let us not grow weary in doing good. For at just the right time we will reap a harvest of blessing, if we don't give up."[1]

I will not live in misery. I will crawl to You if I have to. You will ameliorate my soul.

I love you, Lord.

Amen.

Prayer 86

Lord,

I hope my prayers last.

Lord, I know You have given me grace. But can my grace linger after I am long gone?

I know You do not need me.

I can be replaced, and that is why I am thankful for my existence.

Man is deleterious, but Your power will always be therapy.

Man presents a facade of who he wants us to believe he is, but You, Lord, are the absolute truth.

Peruse me, Lord, and see that I am pure. Examine my heart and taste that I am untainted.

Place me under Your microscope, Lord.

Amen.

Prayer 87

Dear Lord,

It is love. It has always been love. You turn my messes into messages. You turn my tests into testimonies. I am far beyond grateful for You, Lord.

My emotions are lurking, hungry to control me. But Your love will always overcome my emotions.

Jealousy tries to bind me, but my God-given gifts free me. I will be neither Cain nor the prodigal son's older brother.

I will celebrate my brother's winnings as if they were my own.

I will welcome and congratulate my brother with open arms.

His wins are wins for the entire team, and we all will be proud!

Thank you, Lord, for redirecting my emotions.

Amen.

Prayer 88

Dear Lord,

Thank you for Your resurrection; without it, I am doomed.

Your birth, life, death, and resurrection have granted me salvation—a better, eternal life, after this one.

Your deeds are stunningly glorious. You saved me from abortion and childhood trauma. You delivered me from poverty, substance abuse, and addiction.

You have educated me at the best institutions of life. You fed me when I faced malnutrition. You sheltered me and gave me warmth when no loved one could.

You cooled me in blazing fires and kept me afloat in raging seas.

In my paucity of friends, I found You. In my seasons of abundance, I thank You.

In *every* season, I thank You.

Amen.

Prayer 89

Dear Lord,

Please protect me as I travel. I need traveling mercies. Please be seated on all sides of me, covering and shielding me from every impending danger.

You are strong and mighty. Nothing can elude You. You never miss a spot. You are vigilant over every crevice and corner, and I am elated to be Yours. I will be completely and entirely submitted to You.

Guide me every step of the way. I trust You.

Amen.

Prayer 90

Dear Lord,

You are faithful and just. You have shielded me during this short stay away from my home. You have provided another home for me. I have seen and experienced the purpose of my short stay in this place.

Please help me to leave what needs to be left and take with me what must always remain deep within me.

I have learned a great deal. Your presence is direly needed in many places of this life.

Your power is needed in every corner of my existence.

Be a strong foundation, Lord. Be my God. Be my everything. Your aura is potent and it overflows from the surrounding motes.

Amen.

Prayer 91

Dear Lord,

It is rightfully mine. I will not allow myself to be duped by the enemy. I will not allow him to steal my joy. I will not allow myself to be lulled to sleep and cheated out of receiving the manifestations You have revealed to me.

Lord, You are mighty. You bring water, wisdom, and words at the perfect time. You have many prophets and You speak through them in varying ways. You are wondrous. I will never completely understand You. Thank you for Your mysteries. They keep me in awe of Your Glory.

I love You, Lord.

Amen.

Prayer 92

Dear Lord,

Fear has attempted to grab me. And death is waiting at every corner. But I will still continue to trust in You. I will still continue to lean on You. I will find all of my strength in You. And when death comes, I can accept it as is.

Please make me the man I need to be so that I can encourage others. I know You have called me to be a leader, but I fear that I have not experienced enough trials and tribulations to prepare me properly for the liability of leadership. Make me a man, Lord. Give me courage.

I am submitted to You and only to You. Be with me every step of my life, Lord.

This is a fearful time, but I know I can find grace, truth, peace, and comfort in You.

Thank you, Lord.

Amen.

Prayer 93

Dear Lord,

I will closely examine and live according to the adages carefully plotted in Your Book of Proverbs. You give wisdom where there is none. You keep me afloat when my buoyancy has run out. You keep me warm when my temperature has reached zero.

Please show me secrets, Lord. Show me things unknown and untold to man. You are the great revealer, and You give Your children an upper hand. You provide advantages and insights unrivaled.

Lord, show me Your ways. Please lead me, as I lead others.

Give me the love I need to love all that You have placed in my care. I will be kind to them. I will cherish and love each and every one of them. You loved me, so I must be a reflection of Your love.

Thank you, Lord.

Amen.

Prayer 94

Dear Lord,

I work for You. I seek to earn Your Employee of the Month every month. I will pour out my spirit to You. I pray that when my life expires, every bit of my energy has been depleted. I pray that my fountain has run entirely dry. I pray that all my missions are exhausted. I pray.

Lord, I pray that You are pleased with me. I pray that I have fulfilled my calling. I pray that many were delivered, through me, in Your name. I pray.

Amen.

Prayer 95

Lord,

Here I am. I am out in the open for You to do with me as You please. I am at Your mercy. I accept Your grace. I plead for Your forgiveness. My arms are open for Your embrace.

Lord, thank you for all that You are, all that You were, and all that You will be. I know my life is entirely and completely in Your hands.

Lord, I want to be with You wherever You are. Lord, I fear You. Lord, I submit to You. You are my everything, and without You, I am nothing.

Lord, please don't leave my life.

Amen.

Prayer 96

Dear Lord,

Please protect me; I am in the valley of the shadow of death. I cannot do this without You.

But if I should perish, I guess I must perish.

Thank you, Lord, for the time You have given me.

It is a blessing,

Amen.

Prayer 97

Dear Lord,

I wish for my desires to become Your desires. The most terrifying method to life would be to live not according to Your will but according to my own hunger. My way is insignificant when it stands alongside Yours.

I trust You.

Amen.

Prayer 98

Dear Lord,

Draw me closer to You. At times I feel like I am drifting away, getting further and further away from Your presence. I forget that You are my source and that everything I have is a gift from You.

Please continue to show me that my efforts, my skills, and my qualities will never bring the blessings that I desire.

Only You can give blessings. Only You are the gift-giver. You are matchless.

Above You, there is no other. Reprieve me of my pride, cleanse me and wash me.

Please give me wisdom and understanding. Please prune from me everything that needs to be pruned. Please conceal everything on me that needs to be concealed.

I am imperfect and I always will be. But I know that if I stick close to You, Lord, I will be just fine. I will be shielded and protected. I will be made new in You.

In Jesus's name, I pray.

Amen.

Prayer 99

Dear Lord,

Thank you for this day. Thank you for another opportunity to experience life here on Earth. Thank you for being God.

I humbly ask for Your continued guidance. I ask for a double portion of Your grace, truth, wisdom, and understanding. Lord, please help me to see things as You do.

In Jesus's name,

Amen.

Prayer 100

Lord,

Your grace is a guide for my soul. You have chaperones in all four corners of the world, which brings solace to my journey. I can be confident that You will always be good *for* me—especially when my trial does not feel good *to* me.

Lord, I love You. Thank you for life. Thank you for the grace to which I often retreated during my most vulnerable and emotional.

You. Are. Good.

I pray that these prayers would be a vehicle for another, on their journey to their most liberated selves.

I pray that they, too, would develop a relationship with You and experience the same grace that You have offered to me. I pray that they, too, will experience Your love.

You never fail.

For Your glory,

Amen.

Notes

Prayer 8

1. Psalm 37:23

Prayer 9

1. Proverbs 24:16
2. 2 Corinthians 12:9-11

Prayer 11

1. 2 Timothy 1:7

Prayer 19

1. Proverbs 18:21

Prayer 21

1. 2 Corinthians 12:9

Prayer 22

1. Psalm 37:4

Prayer 23

1. Ephesians 4:22-24

Prayer 24

1. 2 Corinthians 12

Prayer 25

1. Joshua 1:9

Notes

Prayer 26

1. Romans 8:26-27

Prayer 28

1. John 8:36

Prayer 31

1. Mark 8:36

Prayer 33

1. Psalm 23:2

Prayer 35

1. 1 John 2:19

Prayer 37

1. Jeremiah 29:13

Prayer 38

1. 2 Corinthians 5:19

Prayer 44

1. John 20:29

Prayer 50

1. Proverbs 13:3

Prayer 64

1. Romans 8:31
2. Isaiah 54:17
3. Psalm 23:5

Prayer 68

1. Matthew 5:3-10

Prayer 81

1. Ephesians 6:11

Prayer 85

1. Galatians 6:9

CPSIA information can be obtained
at www.ICGtesting.com
Printed in the USA
LVHW031105150721
692787LV00001B/79